Brain Power

Transport

from the First Wheels to Special Cars

Penny Clarke

BOOK HOUSE

Contents

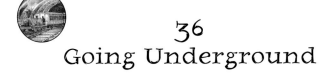

THE FIRST WHEELS

Pre-historic sledge

Imagine a world without wheels! There would be no cars or trucks so there would be little pollution, but no bicycles either. And what about the wheels we don't see – wheels in factories, cog wheels in machines and so on? How would we manage? Probably not as well as our ancestors who built pyramids in Egypt, temples in Greece and Stonehenge in England without the aid of a wheel. In fact, people had been making pottery and transporting heavy goods for centuries before the wheel was invented in about 3000 BC.

2500 BC

Ox cart with a wicker body based on a pottery fragment found in Susa (now part of Iran).

Solid disk wheel

Sumerian Wheel c.3000 BC

A copper tire helps hold the wheel together.

Wheel with copper tire

Early carts had solid wheels. This model of a covered wagon dates from 3000 BC and was found in a tomb in Iraq.

Two Sumerian wheels

Wooden wheel with studs   *Wheel with copper ring*

The first type of wheel was the potter's wheel, thought to have been invented in Sumeria around 5000 BC. It is not known exactly how the wheel's development for transport happened, but without it the world we know today would be very different. Early wheels were very simple: a wooden disk with a hole made for the axle. Wheels allow you to transport heavy items using less energy than if you had to drag them on a sledge.

2500 BC

Limestone carving from Ur in Mesopotamia (now part of Iraq).

Onagers pulling a cart

Fragment of pottery showing a wicker cart (reconstructed above).

We are unsure how these very early wheels worked. Did the wheels rotate around the axle (like modern ones) or did both wheels and axle turn?

Two-wheeled cart (above) reconstructed from a carving found in the ancient city of Ur, Mesopotamia. Onagers (a type of wild donkey) pull it.

War chariot c.2000 BC

Mosaic from Ur showing war chariots pulled by onagers and a reconstruction (right).

Horses cannot pull heavy loads because the harness chokes them.

CHARIOTS FOR WAR

Chariot from Crete c.1400 BC

The first carts had solid wheels. These probably developed from the tree-trunk rollers used for transporting blocks of building stone. Solid wheels are heavy, so vehicles using them are slow and clumsy. Just as we don't know who invented the wheel, we don't know where or when spoked wheels were invented. But the Egyptians were using them by 1475 BC. Wheels with spokes are lighter than solid ones, so the vehicles they support are faster and more manouevrable. At first used by the wealthy for hunting fast animals like gazelles, it was soon realised they would make ideal military vehicles.

A 'bit' between the teeth

Oxen and mules were too slow to pull the new chariots, but horses were ideal. This bronze horse-bit, made in Egypt about 1200 BC, is very like modern ones.

Fast chariot warfare c.1475 BC

It's a two horse power chariot!

Solid wheels are much easier to make than spoked ones, but spoked wheels have so many advantages that they soon replaced them. Making a perfectly round wheel from separate pieces of wood is difficult and requires great skill.

Egyptian wheelrights c.1475 BC *(above)*

Decoration from a chariot in the tomb of Thutmose VI of Egypt, 1420 BC.

The horses carved on this Assyrian frieze from around 850 BC (right) have elaborate bridles and bits in their mouths.

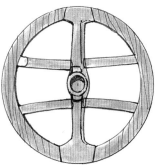

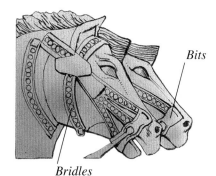

Bits

Bridles

Invasion 1600 BC

Around 1600 BC Egypt was invaded by the Hyksos, a neighbouring people. The invasion was a disaster for the Egyptians because the Hyksos swept in with horses and chariots, neither of which the Egyptians had ever seen. Although routed by the invaders, the Egyptians were quick to learn and soon they, too, had horse-drawn chariots.

This type of 'cross-bar' spoked wheel (above) was used in northern Italy in about 1000 BC and in Greece as shown on this vase (right).

Greek vase from 540 BC showing a wedding procession

A Greek warrior sets off for war in his chariot.

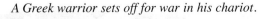

7

ANCIENT CHINA

Chinese coach c.100 BC

Was the wheel invented in the Middle East or China? Or did it evolve separately in both regions? Most scholars now believe Chinese silk merchants who travelled to the Middle East around 1500 BC saw the wheel there and took the idea back to China. What archaeologists are sure of is that the Chinese had better roads than the Romans. Between 1100 and 200 BC the Chinese emperors had ordered a massive programme of road building throughout their lands. Some of the main roads even had special lanes for important traffic!

210 BC

Two-wheeled chariots like this one (below), travelled along China's roads around 210 BC. It is a reconstruction of the chariots archaeologists discovered in tombs in northern China.

The best roads in the world

It's a bargain, sir!

Wheels versus Donkeys!

Wheels are a great invention, but wheeled vehicles are not always practical. They work best on hard, fairly smooth surfaces and routes that aren't too steep. That means building roads. They also need something strong to pull them. That means domesticated animals. But the Silk Road, the great trade route between the Middle East and China, crossed mountains and deserts, so wheeled transport was useless. Instead, merchants continued to use the traditional form of transport – pack animals.

The first emperor c.258 to 210 BC

Bronze model of a Chinese pole-chariot (above) found in the tomb of the emperor, Qin Shihuangdi.

The army of the first Chinese emperor, Qin Shihuangdi (c.258 to 210 BC) had many chariots like the one above. But when archaeologists excavated his tomb, they found no chariots – just the shapes they had left in the ground after they had rotted. From these they were able to reconstruct the emperor's war chariots.

Window grilles

100 BC

Bronze model of a Chinese vehicle dating from 100 BC. Horses were the most expensive animals to use to pull vehicles, so having four suggests the vehicle belonged to a very wealthy person. The fact that this vehicle has a roof and window-grilles also indicates it was used by a very important person or his family. Perhaps the empress or one of the imperial princesses travelled in it. It would certainly have meant ordinary people could not see them. Today, for the same reason, some Chinese officials use cars with lace curtains.

9

ROMAN ROADS

Roman mile stone

Like the Chinese, the Romans established a huge empire. But taking other people's territory is one thing, keeping control of it is quite another. If there is a rebellion, the conquerors need to control it quickly, and that means getting to the troublespot as swiftly as possible. The Romans knew that the best way to do this was to have good roads along which their armies could march fast. They were superb engineers and soon the empire was criss-crossed with roads, many of which still survive under 'modern' roads. Maintaining the roads was expensive, but an essential part of keeping control of the empire. When the empire finally collapsed in AD 476 the roads were no longer used and became neglected.

At the races

Chariot-racing was an exciting and dangerous sport. Controlling four galloping horses needs skill and nerve (above).

"All roads lead to Rome."

A rich woman being carried by slaves in a litter

An early form of public transport. Poorer people could travel between towns in coaches like this one

Are we nearly there yet?

10

Animal shoes

The Romans used iron shoes to protect oxen hooves from the rough road surfaces.

Road works!

The surface of gravel or flat stones, had a camber so rain ran off to stop the road flooding

Surveyors marked out the route of the road

Groma – a device used by Roman surveyors

Labourers dug out the earth and laid the foundation stones on a bed of sand

Layers of chalk, sand and broken bricks went on top. They were beaten flat and firm

A cisium, or light gig that could carry one or two people

11

VIKINGS

Viking cart c.AD 850

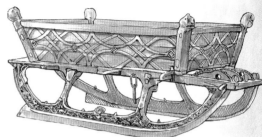

W hat happened to roads and transport in Europe after the Roman Empire collapsed in the 5th century AD? Some regions had no roads anyway because the ground was unsuitable and the Romans had not conquered them. For example, in the Viking homelands of modern-day Scandinavia, the ground is covered with snow and ice for many months, and then becomes waterlogged as it thaws in spring. In these conditions, wheeled vehicles aren't much use – so instead the Vikings used sledges.

c.AD 850

Sledge from c.AD 850 (above) found in a Viking burial mound. The worn runners show it had been used, but the finely carved decoration suggests it was not everyday transport.

Viking ice skates

Hope I'm not skating on thin ice!

Swisssh

Swoosh

Farm cart

The horses pulling this 10th-century French farm cart have collars resting on their shoulders. At last, horses and other animals could pull heavy loads without being half-choked as they did so.

Bone skates

Sledges, with their long smooth runners, travelled quite well over grass and mud, although they were best on snow and ice. The Vikings also used ice skates made from animal bones or reindeer antlers. Using these, they could easily travel long distances over the ice, sometimes pulling a sledge.

c.AD 850

This cart from a Viking burial at Oseberg, Norway, dates from c.AD 850. The fine carving shows it belonged to an important person. But the crude wheels suggest wheeled transport was of little use in mountainous Norway. The cart was one of the finds unearthed from a tomb in 1903. A layer of clay used to seal the tomb helped to preserve the wooden items inside.

Intricate carvings

Finely decorated horse-harnesses (left) they were probably only used on special occasions.

Last journey

The Vikings were great sailors and shipbuilders and many of their most important leaders were buried in ships. The scene below shows how a chief's body might have been taken to his burial. Carried to his ship in a decorated cart, his body was lifted into the ship in the cart's cradle. Then the ship with this last cargo were taken to the burial site.

Corn wagon 1300

THE MIDDLE AGES

Packhorse c.1550

During the Middle Ages (from about the 10th to the 15th centuries) the vehicles on the roads and tracks of Europe changed little. The greatest change was how animals were harnessed to vehicles. The introduction of the padded horse-collar enabled animals to pull much heavier loads. In the past, pairs of horses were harnessed side by side with a pole between them. Now, with the collar round its neck attached to the cart's shafts, one horse could pull a load that had needed two horses before. Why? Because when the horse pulled, the collar and shafts took the strain, instead of the horse's neck as before.

Carts also improved. This one (above) has iron studs in its wheels. They protected the wooden rim and gave a grip on wet ground.

An 11th-century woodcutter loads his cart (above). Even such a simple cart could carry heavier loads than packhorses (top left).

Medieval road rage!

Get out of my way!

At first, shafts were fixed to the body of the cart, making a rigid structure that was difficult to manoeuvre. This problem was solved by making the shafts pivot and move separately from the body of the cart.

The rear horse is between the wagon's shafts and linked to the other horses by ropes running to their collars

Early French passenger carriage 1317

Baggage wagon 1460

Drivers of two-horse vehicles like those above, usually rode the rear horse – much easier than pushing wheelbarrows along rough muddy streets!

Suspension

Early passenger vehicles, were extremely uncomfortable. They had no springs, so the passengers felt every bump and rut in the road. That didn't matter for freight, but it did for passengers. The body of this 14th-century coach (right) is slung from straps to reduce the discomfort.

Wheelbarrow

Although wheelbarrows were invented in ancient China, they do not seem to have been used in Europe until about the Middle Ages. They were only really useful for transporting things over very short distances, for example by miners (left) or porters in towns and cities.

Wheelwright

Wheels had to be strong and flexible to withstand the bad roads. This wheelwright (below) is boring out the hub of a wheel, while an apprentice shapes wood for spokes.

Many carts could be used in a variety of ways. This 13th-century cart (above) could be just a flat platform or have basket-work sides slotted in to take a bigger load. But, however the cart was used, the driver sat on a high seat to give him greater control of his three-horse team.

NOT JUST HORSEPOWER!

Husky dog

Horses and oxen may have been the most commonly used transport animals, especially in Europe, but there are many places where they couldn't survive. Captain Scott, the British polar explorer, was beaten in the race to the South Pole, partly because he used ponies to pull his team's sledges and not dogs like Roald Amundsen, his Norwegian rival. It was too cold for the ponies and their hooves cut into the snow and slipped on the ice. Dogs' paws splay out, spreading their weight and allowing them to gain a better grip on slippery surfaces.

The horses pulling this whirlicote seem to have horse-collars, but are actually harnessed side-by-side in the old way.

A man's best friend is his camel.

Camel train!

Buurrp!

Wheels are often useless in deserts. Camels, which are perfectly adapted for life in deserts, have provided transport throughout Africa, Asia and the Middle East since around 100 BC. Similar to dogs' feet, camels' feet splay out on the loose sand, helping them to grip and travel where nothing else can.

Metal ore

Horse-drawn sledge

In mountainous regions pack dogs carried small, high-value loads like gold or silver ore.

Postillion

Wheelbarrow

Transporting ore in a German mine: a horse-drawn sledge (above) and a wheelbarrow (far right).

The postillion (the rider on the horse) was more comfortable than his passengers. Awkward loads, like barrels of ale, needed someone to steady them.

Horses to America

Horses were taken to North America by Europeans in the 16th century, but the Native Americans had been using the travois (right) for centuries before that, harnessing dogs to pull these sliding load carriers. Similar devices have also been found in Africa.

Travois, a sliding load carrier

Sledge team

A sledge team's harness is quite simple, with a string net that goes over each dog's head. This spreads the strain across the dog's chest when it pulls on the weight.

17

ELEPHANT POWER

The strongest land animals are, of course elephants, and humans have harnessed their strength for thousands of years. The biggest problem for anyone using elephants is water: each one needs up to 225 litres a day! However, that did not stop Hannibal, the Carthaginian general and sworn enemy of the Roman Empire, using elephants when he attacked Rome in 218 BC. He transported them across the Mediterranean Sea from Carthage in North Africa to Spain. From there he led his forces against the Romans. His shock tactics worked and he won some major victories. The elephants tended to panic and stampede in battle, but this made them even more frightening to the enemy soldiers who had probably never seen elephants before.

Elephant builders

When the British Army was building a railway in north-west India in 1858, the engineers designed the train and rail sections to be light enough to carry on the backs of elephants.

When Alexander the Great reached India in 326 BC, his enemy Rajah Porus assembled a huge army that included 100 war-trained elephants! Terrifying in battle, Alexander's army found the best defence was to hack at the elephant's legs to try to cripple them and won the battle.

Elephants at War!

He's just being friendly!

Elephants in armour

Processional elephants

Indian rulers have probably used elephants in their ceremonies since they were domesticated many, many centuries ago. Covered in richly decorated saddle-cloths and with *howdahs* (seats) on their backs, these huge animals created a greater impression of power for the ruler. This illustration of a festival in 1813 (above) shows the Emperor of Delhi and two decorated elephants. In 1876 elephants were used in the same way when Great Britain controlled India and Queen Victoria was proclaimed its Empress.

Elephants in battle armour

Hannibal was not the only general who used elephants in war – many Indian rulers did too. The elephants wore special armour with swords fixed to their tusks. Even when they stampeded, which they often did, the confusion this caused could successfully disrupt an enemy's army.

COACH TRANSPORT

Coachmen c.1790

During the 18th century, people throughout Europe became wealthier. At the same time there were many technical improvements both to roads and the vehicles that travelled on them. One of the greatest improvements, from the passengers' point of view, was the use of plate-glass windows. These first appeared just before 1700 and immediately made journeys more comfortable – for the first time passengers could stay dry if it rained. Then in 1787, John Collinge invented an axle that only needed oiling once a month – before this, axles had to be oiled every day.

Old-fashioned wagons (right) travelled at about 5 km/h.

They were hated by the drivers of the new, faster stagecoaches (right) as they were often in the way.

Trend setter

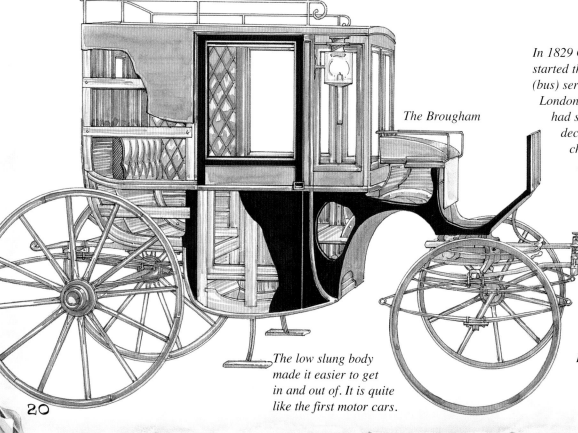

The Brougham

The low slung body made it easier to get in and out of. It is quite like the first motor cars.

In 1829 George Shillibeer started the first omnibus (bus) service (above) in London. Later vehicles also had seats on an open-top deck which were cheaper than the inside seats.

The trend setting Brougham carriage remained popular well into the 1900s. This type of carriage was first built in 1839 for Lord Brougham.

Old fashioned wagon

London to Bath coach

Stagecoach

Phaeton from 1790s

BATH LONDON

GR

At least I don't have to mix with common people.

Sedan chair

The Phaeton was a fast carriage popular with men-about-town in the 1790s. Behind it is a stagecoach. These public coaches carried eight passengers and luggage. In 1784 the London to Bath coach set a record average speed of 11 km/h. To keep up their speed stagecoaches changed horses every 17 km. Horse-drawn transport was not the only way to get around town. Sedan chairs (left) were popular with women. The wealthy had their own, other people hired them.

French is best...for a while

In the mid 17th century the French built the best coaches in Europe (right). But by the 19th century the British had overtaken them.

THE POWER OF STEAM!

Stephenson's America

As far as we know, the ancient Greek, Hero of Alexandria, was the first person to realise the power of steam. In 130 BC he built a model engine which used jets of steam to turn a shaft. This was forgotten until the 18th century. Then, in the 1770s, several engineers built stationary steam engines to power machinery in mines and factories. In the 1780s James Watt made a steam engine which moved a vehicle by using its power to drive a wheel. For over 200 years, miners had transported coal and ore in wagons along trackways, first wooden and then iron. In 1804 the Cornishman Richard Trevithick built a steam engine to run on rails in mines – so starting the railway age.

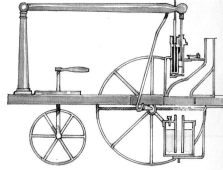

1786

Among the pioneers of steam was William Murdock. In 1786 he built a model steam carriage 0.5 m long. It ran for a distance of 1.5 km.

Stephenson's Rocket!

The boiler on Rocket *was a totally new design. Contact with 25 tubes heated from the firebox created steam. It also had an improved exhaust system.* Rocket *could pull a 14-tonne train at 47 km/h, that was twice as fast as its rivals.*

It's going like a . . . rocket!

1813

In 1813, Christopher Blackett and William Hedley had built *Puffing Billy*, but it was not as efficient as *Rocket*.

George Stephenson (1781-1848) was one of the greatest pioneers of steam engines. He built up a thriving export business, selling different types of steam engine abroad. In 1829 George Stephenson and his son Robert (1803-59) entered Rocket, *the steam locomotive they had designed and built, for the Rainhill (near Liverpool) trials to find the best steam locomotive –* Rocket *won.*

22

1770

Having the boiler in front reduced the risk of fire if either boiler or gun exploded.

In 1770 the French engineer Joseph Cugnot built a military steam wagon to haul heavy guns (below).

Steam coaches

Steam coaches began appearing on Britain's roads in the 1830s. The London to Bath service (below) was the successor of the 1784 record-setting service (page 25).

Stagecoach drivers hated the new steam coaches, saying they terrified their horses. But the real reason was that they were faster, which threatened business.

The first fatal road accident (below) – a steam carriage exploded in Paisley, Scotland, in July 1834.

23

ACROSS A CONTINENT

Pioneers

Although steam-powered vehicles were becoming more common in Europe – the world's first public railway opened in England in 1825 – the situation was very different in North America. After an economic boom on the east coast in the 18th and early 19th centuries, the picture changed. Poverty and unemployment were made worse by a surge of immigrants from Europe. Many families decided to travel westward to seek a better life. They knew there were no roads or even tracks and the people they would meet on their way, the Native Americans, were likely to be hostile. Apart from that, they knew little about where they were going or the conditions they would find there. And to reach this new life they depended on animals.

1860

The Pony Express, a chain of horses and riders to provide a fast mail service across the USA, began in 1860. A year later it was out of business – the electric telegraph made communication faster than any horse and rider.

Across America

Pioneers

The families who set out in search of a new life must have been desperate. They had little idea of what they would find, summers were baking and winters freezing, food and water had to be found as they travelled. A broken wheel was a crisis. They took spares, but time spent changing wheels slowed the convoy – and so did lame animals. If that happened too often, the convoy might not reach the mountains before winter snows made crossing them impossible. Many pioneers died along the way. They travelled in convoys of 20 or more wagons for protection against attack by Native Americans and bandits.

Croak

1869

For those who could afford it, the Wells Fargo Company ran a mail coach service between St Louis, Missouri, and San Francisco, California. The whole journey took 25 days. In 1869 the first railroad across the continent opened, and, like the Pony Express before it, the new form of power took over from coach and horses.

Wells Fargo coach

Schooners

The pioneers' heavy wooden wagons were nicknamed 'prairie schooners'. Weighing over a tonne, they could carry around three tonnes.

I should have left Ma's clock at home.

25

THE AGE OF RAIL TRAVEL

Medal from opening of Belgium-Rhine railway, 1843

During the 18th century someone working in a mine made an important discovery. If the wheels of the wagons had a flange they were less likely to come off the iron rails along which they ran. The wagons also ran more easily, so the wagon horses could pull bigger loads. Flanged wheels were adopted for railways and have been used on them ever since. The 19th century was a time of expansion and optimism. All over Europe and North America entrepreneurs were building businesses, establishing factories and creating trade links at home and abroad. Powering this expansion was the steam engine. Stationary engines drove machines in factories and mobile ones pulled trains carrying passengers and goods across countries and continents.

1831

The 1831 Dewitt Clinton (above) was America's third steam engine. Like stagecoaches, it had seats outside.

East meets West

Yeeeehaw!

Vulcan (above) pulled trains on the Shrewsbury to Birmingham Railway in England in 1849. It has the same wheel arrangement as the European engine on the 1843 medal (far left top).

1869

The worlds first transcontinental railway was started in 1860 in America and aimed to join the Union Pacific and Central Pacific railroads. Union Pacific began laying tracks westward from Omaha, Nebraska and Central Pacific laid tracks eastward from Sacramento, California. On 10 May 1869, the tracks met at Promontory Summit, Utah.

1869

Funnel to prevent stray sparks starting forest fires

Lamp

Carriages on American railways were designed for much longer journeys than European ones.

Passenger cars

Fuel tender

Driver's cab

Boiler

Driving wheels

Leading bogie wheels

Cow-catcher

Stephenson built *North Star (above)*, in 1837 for the Great Western Railway.

Critics of the railways claimed that the trains would kill both plants and wildlife and that the speeds at which they travelled would prevent passengers from being able to breathe!

The Vittorio Emanuele II *(above), named after the first king of united Italy (1870), introduced the 4-6-0 wheel layout.*

Norwegian tank engine, 1870s

Engine of the Tasmanian Government Railway, 1892.

BICYCLES

British velocipede

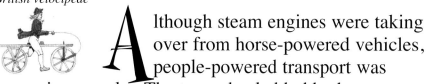

Although steam engines were taking over from horse-powered vehicles, people-powered transport was becoming popular. The two-wheeled hobby horse or velocipede (above) was particularly popular with the French. The earliest hobby horses had no steering, but by 1818, both German and British firms were making hobby horses the rider could steer. By the 1890s bicycles had pneumatic tyres and chains linking the pedals to the rear wheels. With a bicycle you could get out of town at weekends, go touring alone or with one of the many cyclists' touring clubs that came into being. And because there was so little traffic, cycling was a very safe form of transport.

1839

Kirkpatrick MacMillan, a Scottish blacksmith, made the first real bicycle in 1839.

Now, how do I make it stop?

Penny Farthing

shake

rattle

1870

The wooden-wheeled velocipede or 'Boneshaker' of 1870. The pedals were fixed to the front-wheel spindle. The name 'Boneshaker' is often used to refer to bicycles before the invention of the pneumatic tyre.

'Ordinaries' or 'Penny Farthings' had a step on their frame to help riders vault into the saddle. It was invented by James Starley in 1871 and named after two British coins of the time: the penny which was large, and the farthing which was much smaller. It had a tubular metal frame and rubber tyres and due to the distance between the saddle and the pedals, only those with long legs could ride it.

Tandem

Tandem bicycle

For those women who had time and money for the hobby, bicycling gave a newfound independence. Tandem bicycles have two seats and two sets of pedals but only one frame.

Bicycle school

Riding a bicycle took skill. In Europe and North America schools sprang up to teach those skills.

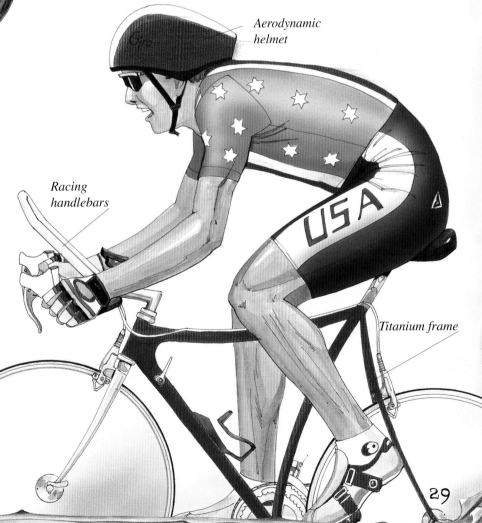

Aerodynamic helmet

Racing handlebars

Titanium frame

Light bikes

In contrast to the heavy metal frames of the 19th-century bicycles, modern racing bikes use new high-tech materials to make strong, light bicycles. Frames are made of titanium and the wheels are discs of carbon-fibre.

Racing bike

29

Speed on Two Wheels

Michaux steam-bike

Adding an engine to a bicycle was the next step, just as it had been to horseless carriages – and would be in later years to gliders. In 1869 the French Michaux brothers added a steam engine to their bicycles (above). These first 'motorcycles' could go for 16 km without refuelling. But as the rider sat over the boiler, which was both hot and dangerous, it was not very popular. In 1885 the German engineer Gottlieb Daimler designed a wooden bicycle with a petrol engine (right). It too, was not very successful. The real breakthrough was in 1894 when the German-made twin-cylinder Hildebrand und Wolfmüller reached 38 km/h – faster than most cars of the time!

1885

The Reitwagen (above) was built by Gottlieb Daimler in 1885. Unfortunately it was very slow, and someone walking briskly could almost keep up with it!

First motorbikes

Putt

Putt

Clank

1905

Motorbikes were much cheaper than cars, so quickly became popular. And improved engine designs made them even faster. As motorcycle engines got better, the machines they powered became faster throughout the early 20th century. Harley-Davidsons still use V-twin engines – first introduced in 1905.

German DKW, 1921

USA, Ner-a-Car, 1921

USA, Harley-Davidson, 1916

In 1904 the Belgian FN motorbikes introduced four-cylinder engines. These were far in advance of their time – it is multi-cylinder designs that have made Japanese motorbikes so successful.

Belgian, four-cyclinder FN, 1904

BMW produced many fine motorcycles. Launched in 1938, the 500cc R51 (below) had a horizontal cylinder on each side of the engine. Known as a 'flat twin' engine, this design is still used in today's BMW motorbikes.

As motorcycles got faster, so racing them grew in popularity. In 1926 Jimmy 'Machine Buster' Simpson (above), riding an AJS, reached speeds of over 110 km/h on the Manx TT (Tourist Trophy) circuit. This legendary motorbike race held annually on the Isle of Man now regularly sees speeds over 190 km/h as bikes have developed.

THE MOTOR CAR ARRIVES

Rickett's three-wheel steamer

A t the same time as he was developing motor-cycles, Gottlieb Daimler was experimenting with petrol engines in cars. He and Karl Benz, another German engineer, had both developed internal combustion engines suitable for road vehicles. In 1885 both men produced road vehicles driven by petrol engines – the ancestors of every car and lorry on the road today. Benz's 'car' looked more like a tricycle, while Daimler's vehicle looked much more like a horse-drawn carriage, but without the horses. Peugeot, a French company, bought the rights to use Daimler engines, and soon the first Peugeot cars appeared on French streets.

1873

Amédée Bollée's steam carriage (above) of 1873 and similar vehicles powered by batteries were smooth and quiet – unlike the early noisy, smelly petrol-driven vehicles.

The first car, 1888

1885

Karl Benz's first petrol-powered vehicle (above) was built in 1885. Benz's 1888 model (left) was the very first motor car to be seen in England. Both vehicles were modelled on popular types of horse-drawn carriage.

Four-stroke engines

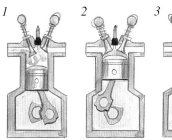

1   2   3   4

Not one of my most attractive outfits!

How four-stroke engines work:
1) Valve sucks air and fuel into cylinder.
2) Valve closes. Piston compresses the mixture.

3) Spark ignites the mixture. This expands, pushes piston down to turn wheels.
4) Another valve opens. Piston pushes out waste gases and the cycle begins again.

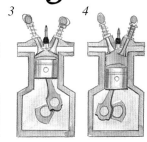

Panhard et Levassor, 1895

Peugeot Phaeton, 1894

Pessey electric car, 1897

Motorists needed extra clothes to keep them warm and dry. Dust was a problem when the weather was dry, and when it rained, mud would often splatter passengers. Women wore facemasks to protect their faces from the wind and goggles to protect against grit and dirt.

1894-1895

Early cars looked like the horse-drawn carriages they were replacing. Both the 1895 Panhard et Levassor (above left) and 1894 Peugeot (above) went faster with their hoods down. This showed the importance of streamlining vehicles to reduce wind-resistance.

L'Eléphant, *a British electric car (right), took part in the 1898 Paris – Amsterdam race.*

1896

The American engineer Henry Ford (right) built his first car in 1896. Like all early cars it looked like a horse-drawn carriage, but instead of being pulled by a horse it was powered by a petrol-driven internal combustion engine.

33

BUSES, TRAMS & LORRIES

London tram c.1902

From about 1890 to the beginning of World War One in 1914, all transport was powered in one of four ways: horses, electricity, steam or petrol. All had advantages and disadvantages. Horses were expensive and needed fuel (food) even when not working. Electric vehicles, like the London tram of 1902 (above), were quiet, but their heavy electric batteries needed recharging frequently (as they still do). Steam was ideal for large vehicles like railway engines, but not so great working in confined places like city streets was much more difficult.

1830

In the 1830s, Harlem and New Orleans in America, introduced horse-drawn public trams. By pulling tramcars on rails the horses could pull more passengers at faster speeds. The horses then became passengers for the downhill run.

London B-type Omnibus

Getting across London has never been easier!

1890

The Cincinnati grip car of 1890 was hauled by a cable running back to the engine shed. This method was only useful for short journeys, generally in hilly places.

1910

In 1910 the petrol-powered B-type omnibus (left) started carrying passengers in London. This simple but reliable, model was used for the world's first bus fleet.

Steam-powered traction engine

Trams are once again regarded as a good form of public transport because they are quiet and environmentally friendly.

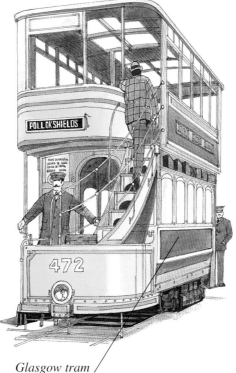

Steam wagons like the 1906 Sentinel (above) were very reliable. But petrol lorries proved easier to start and drive, and used less fuel.

Trolleybus

Transport's past and future (above). An old-fashioned, steam-powered traction engine and trailer off-loads tram rails. These will be used by vehicles like the tram (right) which ran in Glasgow from 1903 to 1959. Trams that got electricity from overhead wires (invented in 1881 by Werner von Siemens) did not need to recharge their batteries.

Glasgow tram

Trolleybuses (above), like trams, got electricity via overhead wires, but having wheels are more useful in cities.

Brewer's steam wagon

Sentinel steam lorry, 1910

Trams are more common in Europe than the UK

The red double-decker bus quickly became an iconic symbol of London

Smaller buses, such as this 1948 Daimler, were used on country routes

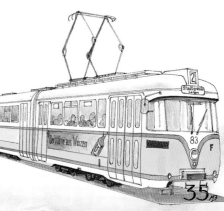

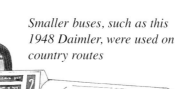

MADAME TUSSAUDS

GOING UNDERGROUND

Poster for London's Underground, 1927

A completely new form of transport opened to the public in London in 1863: the world's first underground railway: the Metropolitan Railway. It was designed to link London's mainline stations, such as Paddington, Waterloo and Liverpool Street, which were then on the outskirts of London, and take passengers into central London. The tunnels were made by the 'cut and cover' method: deep trenches lined with bricks were covered with reinforced roofs to support the buildings and roads above the tunnels.

Underground mail

In London, the Royal Mail built an underground railway (above) to take mail between the central sorting office and the main railway stations.

On the move underground

1908

The 'cut and cover' building method could only be used on land not already built over – difficult to find in big cities. But in the 1880s the engineer, J. H. Greathead designed a tunnelling shield. Men inside a strong metal tube dug out the tunnel. The shield stopped the tunnel falling in on them. As the shield moved forward, the tunnel behind it was supported by tubular iron linings – from which comes the underground's nickname 'the tube'. London's underground was so successful that other countries soon built their own. In 1900 two more European capital cities got undergrounds: Paris (France) and Budapest (Hungary). In 1904 New York's subway (underground) opened.

36

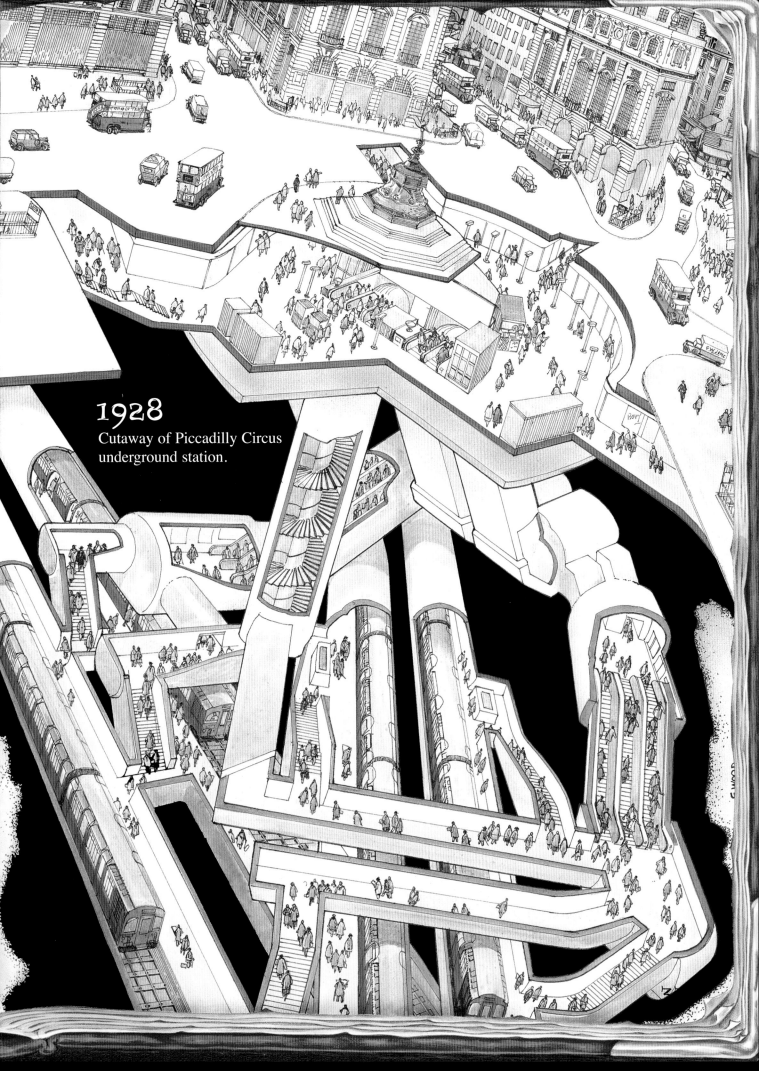

1928
Cutaway of Piccadilly Circus
underground station.

MASS-PRODUCING CARS

Rolls-Royce, 1905

The first cars were enormously expensive. They were handmade from the finest materials in the same way that the best horse-drawn carriages had been made. They were status symbols for the wealthy and the car that reflected this best was a Rolls-Royce (top left). These cars were a partnership between Henry Royce and the Honourable C. S. 'Charlie' Rolls. Royce had the engineering skills and Rolls had the wealthy friends who could afford such cars. But there was another way of producing cars, which was taken by American Henry Ford. Although Ford's first cars were handmade, he wanted to make cars that were cheap enough for everyone to own. To do this he developed mass production and a process that would later be called 'Fordism'.

Rolls   Royce

C.S. Rolls (1877-1910)   *Henry Royce (1863-19[...]*

1908

In 1908, only three years after their first car, the Type 70 Rolls-Royce (below) won the Gold Medal for reliability at the RAC Scottish Trial over 3,218 km.

Steam car

Condenser

Boiler

1903

The 1903 White Steamer used a petrol-fired boiler. To make the water last longer, the radiator condensed steam from the engine. Steam cars gave a quieter, smoother ride than petrol cars of the time.

Industrialists from all over Europe went to see Ford's factories in Detroit. In 1916 Fiat, the Italian car maker, built a factory at Lingotto (below) based on Ford's factories. It even had a roof-top test-track.

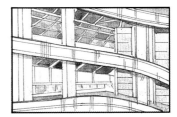

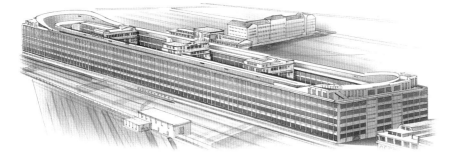

Fiat's Lingotto factory: spiral ramps (above) linked the production floors.

Fiat 501s coming off the assembly line in 1924 —

Henry Ford!

'Fordism' was the term given to the manufacturing methods Henry Ford introduced. It was quite revolutionary, and since then has been adapted for many other industries. Now many modern cars are made mainly by robots.

Ford Model T

Like Royce, Henry Ford (1863-1947) taught himself engineering. He wanted to make cars, like the Model T (right), that most people could afford. To do this he created simple designs and developed production lines to take car parts to the workers.

CARS FOR THE PEOPLE

Auto Union designed by Porsche, 1934

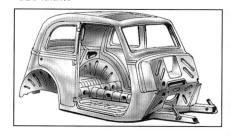

Henry Ford's methods proved so successful that soon other car makers started mass-producing cars. But the market for cars was still quite small because they were expensive. Even the Model T Ford, which was designed to be cheap, cost $850 when it reached the showrooms in 1908. And $850 was a year's wages for a farm or factory worker. But, thanks to mass production, a Model T cost $260 by 1925. The first cheap small cars were based on motorcycle engines and nicknamed 'cyclecars'. They were very light and often had hand-lever controls like a motorcycle's. Then in 1922, came the British Austin Seven. Although intended for the mass market, it was designed like a big luxury car.

The 1922 Morgan three-wheeler cyclecar was so light it could reach 128 km/h.

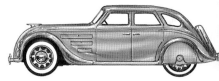

Early cars had a body fitted to a chassis (below right). With mass-production, the two were combined in a rigid welded steel 'box'. Above is the body of a 1938 H-type Vauxhall.

Volkswagen - people's car

This 1934 Chrysler Airflow was a rich man's car. Its new streamlined bodyshape was unpopular at first, but soon caught on.

The Volkswagen or 'people's car' (left), designed by Ferdinand Porsche on the orders of Hitler. Hitler wanted cheap family cars to be widely available to Germans. Porsche also designed the 1934 Auto Union (top left).

KRV 714

British Austin Seven, 1925

French Amilcar, 1925

In the 1920s the motorcyle and sidecar were the cheapest form of personal motor transport.

Morris Minor, 1928

The UK's MG K3 Magnette, 1933, a fast small sports car.

The French car manufacturer Citröen introduced many innovative car designs. This 1934 model had front-wheel drive.

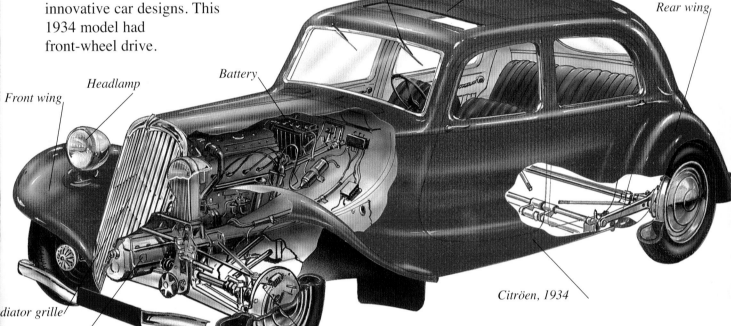

Windscreen wipers

Sliding sunroof

Rear wing

Battery

Headlamp

Front wing

diator grille

Gearbox

Number plate

Front brakes

Citröen, 1934

Wood frame

When the car's wooden frame (above) was finished, it was fitted to the chassis and then covered in aluminium panels.

Steel chassis

This is how the first cars were built. The chassis (below) was made of U-section steel rails and the engine, springs, axles and gearbox were mounted on it. Then the body was fitted to the chassis (below).

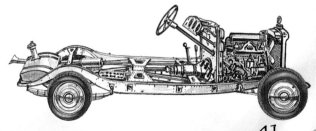

WAR!

Welbike folding scooter

Soviet GAZ-AAA truck, 1939

World War Two began in September 1939. It was only 21 years since World War One had ended, but the two wars would be fought in very different ways. German military planners, in particular, realised that motor transport would give them great opportunities for fast, surprise attacks – a manoeuvre known as *blitzkrieg* or 'lightning war.' There would be no more lines of trenches, with the enemies making little progress as they fought it out for years. Instead, waves of powerful tanks would smash through enemy defences, backed-up by aircraft and motorised troop transporters. Soon the motor industries of the countries involved, Germany, Britain and Russia, and the USA from 1941, were producing vehicles for military use.

The Soviet (Russian) GAZ-AAA truck, based on the 1928 Model A Ford, was old-fashioned but very tough.

Leyland 3-tonne truck (above) painted for desert warfare. Many army trucks were just ordinary trucks adapted for military use.

Unlike the slow, unreliable tanks of World War One, the new ones were formidable fighting machines. They had relatively thin armour and small-calibre guns so were still vulnerable to air attacks. The Panther was designed as a counter-measure to the highly successful Soviet tank, the T34. The Panther was first used in 1943 and carried a crew of 5. It was armed with a 75-mm calibre main gun and twin MG34 machine guns.

German Panther tanks

Bedford ambulance, 1940

Tanker used to refuel fighter aircraft, 1940

Despatch rider, 1942

Bedford military truck, 1939

US Army Jeep, 1940

Military vehicles

The 1939 military truck and 1940 ambulance were made by Bedford, a British truck manufacturer. The truck could transport troops, ammunition or supplies. The ambulance carried four stretcher cases or ten seated wounded. The 1940 US Jeep became world-famous. Its name stands for General Purpose (GP) vehicle, because that is how it was used. It was even converted, not very successfully, into an amphibious vehicle (below).

German officials used luxury cars like the Mercedes-Benz 320 (below).

The Volkswagen's rear-wheel drive gave its wheels a good grip on surfaces like sand. Field Marshal Rommel used it in the desert war in North Africa (1941-43).

1944

British Army despatch riders landing in France on D-Day, 6 June 1944 (above). Paratroops were dropped with folding motorscooters (opposite top).

The 1930s Volkswagen was redesigned as a military vehicle during World War Two (above). Its original designer, Ferdinand Porsche, gave it an easy-to-make slab-sided body.

1930

The Volkswagen 82 converted into a *kübelwagen*, an open-topped military vehicle similar to a jeep.

43

RAILWAY TRANSPORT

Gordon Highlander, *1900*

The 1930s and 1940s were the golden age of steam railway transport. Cars were too expensive for most people and cheap air travel was still years ahead in the future. The fastest, most powerful steam locomotives were built in this period. But they had disadvantages: they caused pollution, needed skilled drivers and had to take on water and coal at regular intervals. Fuel and water supplies caused particular difficulties on long-distance routes such as crossing North America. New locomotives with diesel engines were developed to overcome the problem: they could cross the USA on a single tank of fuel. Electric locomotives, which caused no pollution, were useful on busy routes in built-up areas.

Streamlined steam engines (above) could reach 160 km/h on the London to Scotland routes.

Pantograph

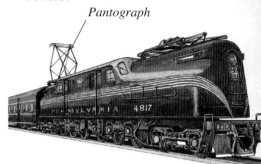

1934 American 7,500 electric locomotive. The pantograph (above) picked up the electric current from overhead wires.

1950s Pacific steam engine

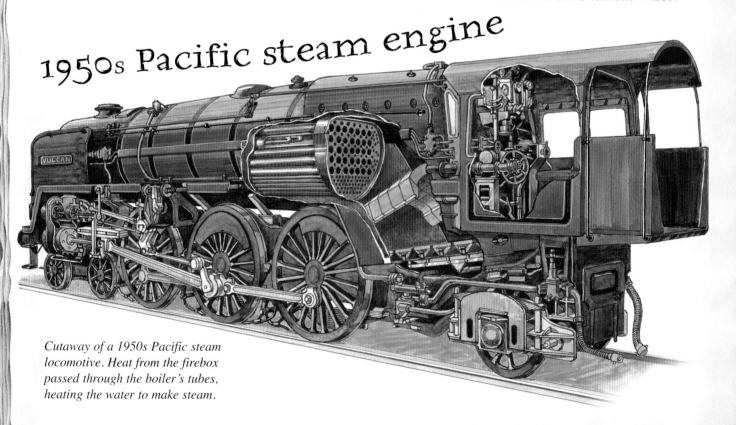

Cutaway of a 1950s Pacific steam locomotive. Heat from the firebox passed through the boiler's tubes, heating the water to make steam.

Largest trains!

The 500-tonne Big Boys, the largest locomotives ever built, pulled trains of 5,000 tonnes over the 4,000 m high Rocky Mountains in North America.

Railways are no longer the most popular method of transport over long distances. In countries like the USA and Canada, with huge distances between east and west coasts, flying costs about the same as rail – and is always quicker! Even in small European countries it is often cheaper and quicker to fly.

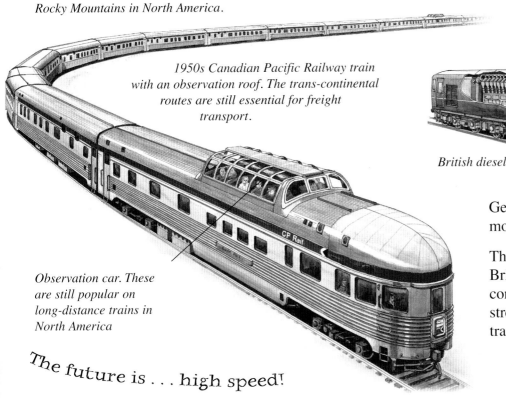

1950s Canadian Pacific Railway train with an observation roof. The trans-continental routes are still essential for freight transport.

Observation car. These are still popular on long-distance trains in North America

British diesel

Generators drive the electric motors in diesel-electrics.

The blunt-nosed design of the British and Canadian trains contrasts sharply with the streamlined high-speed trains below.

The future is . . . high speed!

If railways are to have a future as long-distance passenger transport, the answer is to make the journey-time shorter. Some countries have introduced high-speed trains. Japan has run Bullet trains (right) since 1965. Streamlined in design, they are well soundproofed and passengers sit in airline-style seats. Germany has the ICE, and France the TGV. The drawback is that they are expensive to introduce as they need special rolling-stock and rails.

Bullet train, Japan

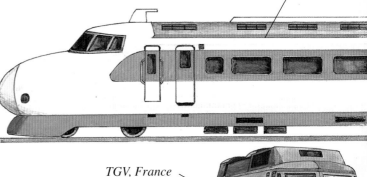

TGV, France

ICE (Inter City Express), Germany

45

HAULING FREIGHT

Articulated lorry

As internal combustion engines became more powerful and reliable, the vehicles they could power got bigger too. And as the vehicles got bigger, so did the loads they carried. Railways could not compete with road transport for delivering goods in towns and cities. In fact many railway companies also had fleets of trucks and vans – horse-drawn at first – to deliver goods (that came by rail) to shops and factories. Today we think of trucks and vans as having diesel engines, but that wasn't always true. At first, steam-powered vehicles were more reliable and cheaper to run than those with petrol engines. But in the 1930s reliable diesel engines were developed and put in goods vehicles, which have used them ever since.

1912

Foden built steam delivery vehicles until 1931. This 1912 lorry carried a 4-tonne load. But look how small its load area is compared with that of the truck (top left).

Truckers

Twin exhausts

Driver's cab is set back from heat of engine

Rest cabin

Truck made by the US Marmon company founded in 1902. The twin exhausts run up each side of the cab.

Opel-Blitz, Germany

Many lorry designs were very adaptable. This German-made Opel-Blitz 3-tonne truck was introduced in the early 1930s. During World War Two it became a four-wheel-drive army truck and in the 1950s appeared as a fire engine.

Customised vehicles

Some manufacturers would sell a vehicle's chassis for a company to add the body – ideal for companies wishing to customise their vehicles. The chassis of the 1925 Morris Commercial (right) cost £172.

Articulated lorries or 'artics' (above) come in two parts: traction unit (tractor) and the freight carrier coupled to it. While goods are unloaded, it can be uncoupled and the driver can go to another job.

Trains on the road

Huge road trains take goods across a country's vast areas without roads. In the days before road trains, camels were often used as transport across Australia's desert areas.

Driving there is dangerous and almost every year people die when their vehicles break down.

Terex 33-11B

Pass any big road-building site and there will be huge off-road earth-movers like the Terex 33-11B (above). The driver's cab is so high off the ground he climbs a ladder to reach it.

CARS BIG AND SMALL

Messerschmitt Tiger, 1953

General Motors Firebird III, 1958

Bond Minicar, 1949

The American economy boomed after World War Two. Most people had jobs, and wages were high. Instead of making military vehicles like tanks, trucks and planes, manufacturers switched to goods for civilians. And among the most popular of these goods were cars. The big, bold styles of American cars built in the 1950s reflect the country's prosperity and confidence. Things were different in Europe. Large areas of the continent had been devastated by the fighting, food was still in short supply and construction materials had to be used to rebuild the homes and factories destroyed in the war. European cars of the time reflected these differences. Unlike the American models, they were smaller, more modest vehicles – and used far less fuel.

All the cars above reflect Europe's economic situation in the decades following World War Two, they were small and, at first, cheap to build. The 1949 three-wheel Bond Minicar was powered by a two-stroke motorcycle engine.

1964

One of the most famous cars in the world is the Aston Martin DB5 driven by James Bond in the 1964 film, Goldfinger. Fitted with many exciting gadgets, Sean Connery as 007 was able to flip a button on the gearstick and eject his unwelcome passenger. The car was also fitted with a bulletproof windscreen, oil slick and smoke screen dispensers, revolving number plates and two machine guns!

Bòiinng

I hope he has a head for heights!

Aston Martin

JB 007

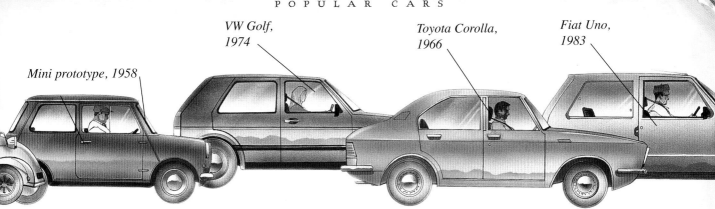

Mini prototype, 1958

VW Golf, 1974

Toyota Corolla, 1966

Fiat Uno, 1983

Another inexpensive car was Messerschmitt's 1953 two-seater Tiger bubble car. But the most revolutionary small car was the Mini of 1958. Designed to seat four people, it destroyed the market for bubble cars and other economy vehicles.

The Mini's popularity led other manufacturers to design small cars. Volkswagen introduced the Golf (above) in 1974 to replace the Beetle. About this time Japan began exporting cars, like the Toyota Corolla (above), to Europe.

Citröen 2CV

'The snail'

The French Citröen 2CV (nicknamed the 'snail') was probably the most popular of all small cars. It was made from 1949 until 1989 (above).

Pontiac Silver Streak

The Pontiac Silver Streak (below) from 1948 shows the big, bold, and confident look of post-war American cars. The 'streak' in the name referred to the chrome grill that featured on the hood of the car.

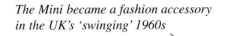

The 'streak'

Whitewall tyres

Chrome bumper

Mini

Alec Issigonis (1906-1988) designed both the Morris Minor and the Mini. The brilliance of his design for the Mini lay in having a front-wheel drive and a transverse engine. Although it was small, this design gave the Mini the performance of a much larger car.

The Mini became a fashion accessory in the UK's 'swinging' 1960s

49

1935

Malcolm Campbell was the first to reach 483 km/h on land, in 1935.

1907

Glenn Curtiss's bike used an aircraft engine to reach 220 km/h in 1907.

1899

The Belgian Camille Jenatzy in his electric car in 1899, the first vehicle to exceed 100 km/h.

Brake chute

Rear wheel steering

SPEED

Thrust SSC

The land speed record is the greatest prize in motoring – its holder is the fastest person on Earth. The current record of 1,227 km/h, set on 15 October 1997, by the *Thrust* supersonic car, is also the world's first supersonic land speed record. The earliest land speed record cars were electric and steam vehicles, but petrol engines soon took over, dominating the record for decades. As record speeds climbed, the shape of the cars became more important. By the 1930s, cars were long and narrow, so that they would accelerate through the air more easily. In the 1960s, land speed challengers used engines to achieve greater speeds with jet thrust.

Disc brakes

1997

Thrust SSC was driven by Royal Airforce pilot, Andy Green. It was powered by two Rolls-Royce Spey jet engines that are normally used on fighter planes. It was as powerful as 1,000 family cars, or 140 Formula 1 racing cars.

1970

Richard Noble set the official land speed record, or LSR of 1,019 km/h in his jet-powered aluminium-wheeled car Thrust 2 *in 1978.*

1978

Gary Gabelich was the first to reach 1,000 km/h, in 1970 in his rocket-powered Blue Flame.

THE BLUE FLAME

INITIAL SERVICES

IMI NorgrenEnots **THRUST 2**

turbo

Kawasaki

1964

Donald Campbell in Proteus Bluebird, *was the first to reach 644 km/h on land, a record he set in 1964.*

1978

Don Vesco (above) on his 'streamliner' bike, Lightning Bolt, *set a world motorcycle speed record of 512 km/h in 1978.*

Supercat all-terrain vehicle

Body shell made from aluminium, carbon-fibre and titanium.

Supersonic cars

Thrust SSC (Supersonic car) blasted its way into the record books in the Black Rock Desert in the USA, its 100,000 horsepower engines at full power. Black Rock was chosen because it is one of the few places on Earth that is big enough and flat enough for a car to accelerate to more than 1,000 km/h.

Welded T45 steel space frame

JAPANESE SPEEDSTERS

Motorbike enthusiasts

Shock absorbers

As Europe struggled to rebuild after World War Two, motorbikes, sometimes with sidecars, were the only form of personal transport that many people could afford. Most of the motorbikes however, were unreliable and noisy – just like the pre-war ones. Then came Japanese bikes. In 1960 Honda designed and built the 250cc Honda Dream. It could reach 152 km/h, a speed beyond all but the most expensive European motorbikes. Within 10 years Honda had sold nearly a million motorbikes in Europe, and other Japanese makers followed. Few European manufacturers could match the Japanese on quality or cost, and many went out of business. Japanese high-performance bikes also came to dominate motorcycle racing.

Front brakes

Valentino Rossi

Zoooom

2005

Valentino Rossi (nicknamed 'The Doctor') is the reigning MotoGP World Champion. He won his 7th World Championship title in just 10 years in 2005. This achievement includes winning the MotoGP every year since 2001.

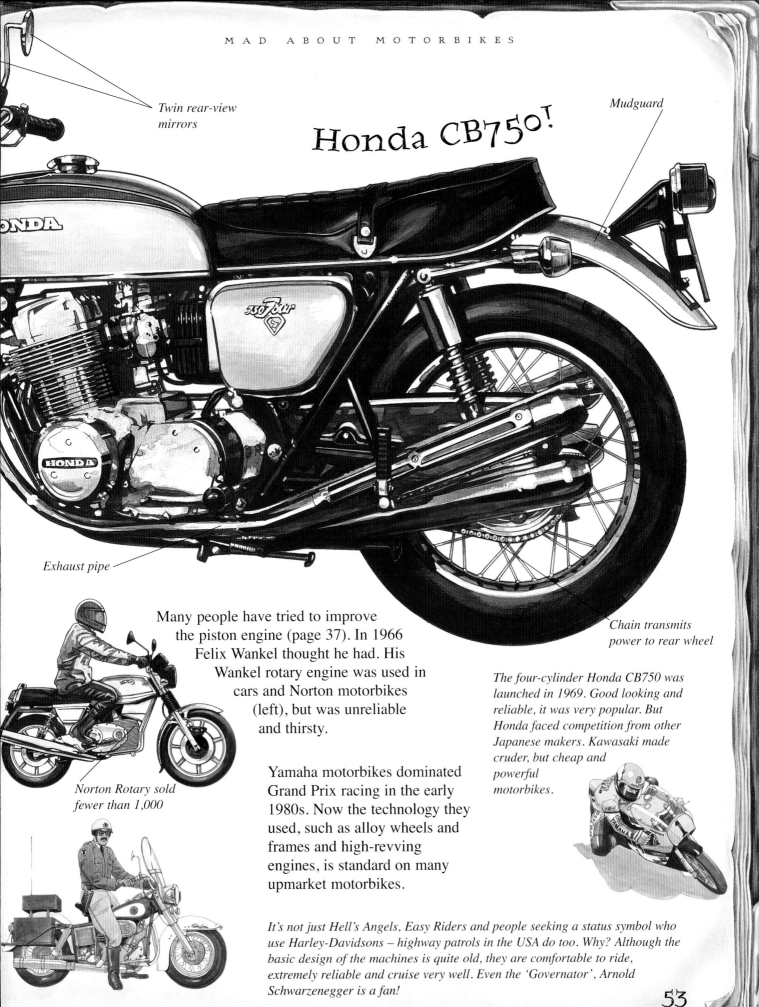

Twin rear-view mirrors

Mudguard

Honda CB750!

Exhaust pipe

Chain transmits power to rear wheel

Many people have tried to improve the piston engine (page 37). In 1966 Felix Wankel thought he had. His Wankel rotary engine was used in cars and Norton motorbikes (left), but was unreliable and thirsty.

Norton Rotary sold fewer than 1,000

The four-cylinder Honda CB750 was launched in 1969. Good looking and reliable, it was very popular. But Honda faced competition from other Japanese makers. Kawasaki made cruder, but cheap and powerful motorbikes.

Yamaha motorbikes dominated Grand Prix racing in the early 1980s. Now the technology they used, such as alloy wheels and frames and high-revving engines, is standard on many upmarket motorbikes.

It's not just Hell's Angels, Easy Riders and people seeking a status symbol who use Harley-Davidsons – highway patrols in the USA do too. Why? Although the basic design of the machines is quite old, they are comfortable to ride, extremely reliable and cruise very well. Even the 'Governator', Arnold Schwarzenegger is a fan!

53

FOUR-WHEEL RACERS

Bentley c.1925

Since the car's earliest days, racing has been one of the world's most popular sports. But today's races, between cars you can barely see as they pass, are very different from the first motor race. Held in France in 1895, drivers travelled 1200 km from Paris to Bordeaux and back. Emile Levassor won because his car didn't break down! A Peugeot came second, arriving six hours later – a contrast with today's split-second timings! A motor racing craze swept Europe. Races were held on public roads, with frequent deaths and injuries. To make the races fairer, formulae (rules) specifying sizes and weights for the cars were introduced in 1902 and this is where the 'formula' in Formula 1 comes from.

The town of Le Mans, France, hosts an annual 24-hour race. First held in 1923, British Bentleys (top left) won it five times between 1924 and 1930.

The badges of two motor-racing teams: Lotus, UK (left) and Ferrari, Italy (right). The C in the Lotus badge represents Colin Chapman, the firm's founder. As young men, both he and Enzo Ferrari had raced.

2005

Motor racing is a young(ish) man's sport. Young drivers lack experience and stamina. But the split-second reactions racing drivers rely on, get slower with age – just like everyone else's. But for top drivers, like Michael Schumacher who drives for Ferrari (left), the danger is worth the rewards. Schumacher has been World Champion 7 times, but lost his title to Fernando Alonso in 2005.

Michael Schumacher

Every February in Florida one of the world's most famous races takes place: the Daytona 500. The cars look more like 'ordinary' cars than those in Grand Prix races, but their engines definitely aren't ordinary. The Daytona 500 is run by NASCAR (National Association for Stock Car Auto Racing) over a track 4 km long.

Rallying is another popular motor sport, but in these races the cars race against the clock, not each other. Drivers and cars are tested over different types of terrain. A navigator helps the driver. The two communicate via intercoms in their helmets.

When this Porsche GT1 won the 1998 Le Mans 24-hour race, it was the company's sixteenth victory and marked its domination of the race. It would be very dangerous for one driver to stay behind the wheel for the whole race, so two or three drivers take turns to drive the same car.

55

THE DESIGN REVOLUTION

Creating a new car

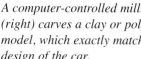

Early car makers would be amazed if they could see how today's cars are made. Some things however, don't change: every new design begins with an idea. It's the process of turning that idea into a car that has undergone a revolution. Once, every car maker had a huge drawing office, where hundreds of skilled draughtsmen (and it was usually men) drew every aspect of a new design, and then redrew the plans when it was modified. Models built from the plans were tested and modified. Then full-size prototypes were made, tested, and again modified. Finally, often years later, the car went into production. Today, thanks to computers, everything can be done on screen in a fraction of the time.

First, a new design is sketched

Computer aided design

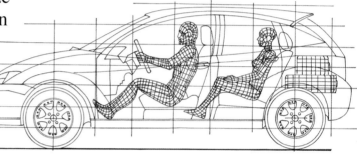

Step 1

The designer, briefed about the new model, sketches his ideas on paper (top). When these are approved, a CAD (computer aided design) programme translates ideas into reality and checks it meets safety requirements.

Step 2

A computer-controlled milling machine (right) carves a clay or polystyrene model, which exactly matches the design of the car.

Built by robots

Robots can build cars with absolute accuracy 24 hours a day, every day.

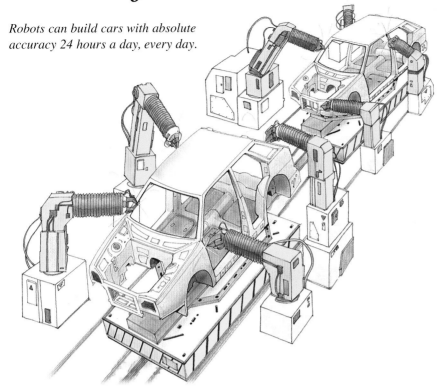

Step 3

Once the new model's general shape is agreed, details of its interior, and 'people', are added on the computer.

Step 4

Adding colour, lighting and shadows to the image on the screen gives a realistic image of the finished car.

On the car production line (above), robots are 'spot-welding' car body shells. Two copper rods squeeze the pieces being joined. A powerful electric current runs between them, melting the steel and joining it together.

Step 5

Testing the car's shape in a wind tunnel (left). A powerful stream of air is blown at a full-size prototype. Coloured smoke in the air shows how the air flows over the car. If the air flow is uneven, the shape needs modifying. When everyone is satisfied, the car goes into production. Then there will be more checks before it finally goes on sale.

Best-seller!

The finished product

The Ford Focus was launched in 1998 and has won over 60 awards, including 'Car of the Year' in both Europe and America. It is now one of the best-selling cars in the world.

AIR POLLUTION

Venturi Fétish

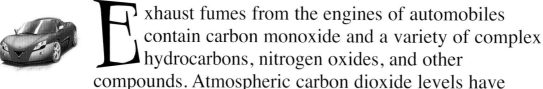

Exhaust fumes from the engines of automobiles contain carbon monoxide and a variety of complex hydrocarbons, nitrogen oxides, and other compounds. Atmospheric carbon dioxide levels have increased steadily since 1900, and the rate of increase is accelerating and creating a 'greenhouse effect'. This means that light can escape, but heat is trapped inside Earth's atmosphere. An increase in carbon dioxide therefore, is causing an increase in the temperature of Earth's atmosphere. This could cause the polar ice caps to melt, raising the sea level, and flooding the coastal areas of the world. But efforts to reduce pollution from car engines and to develop pollution-free engines may eventually eliminate the more serious air pollution problems. Use of fuels that are low in pollutants, such as low-sulphur forms of petroleum is one method that can be used for controlling pollution, another is exploring new technology to create electric cars.

Battery powered

The exotically named Fétish (below) from the French manufacturer Venturi, is the world's first electric sportscar. It has a maximum speed of 170 km/h and each car is made to order. It's powered by a revolutionary lithium-ion battery that needs to be recharged every 350 km. However the price is high, with each car selling for about £400,000.

2005

2005
Nissan Pivo

Powered by a lithium-ion battery, the Nissan Pivo creates no emisssions.

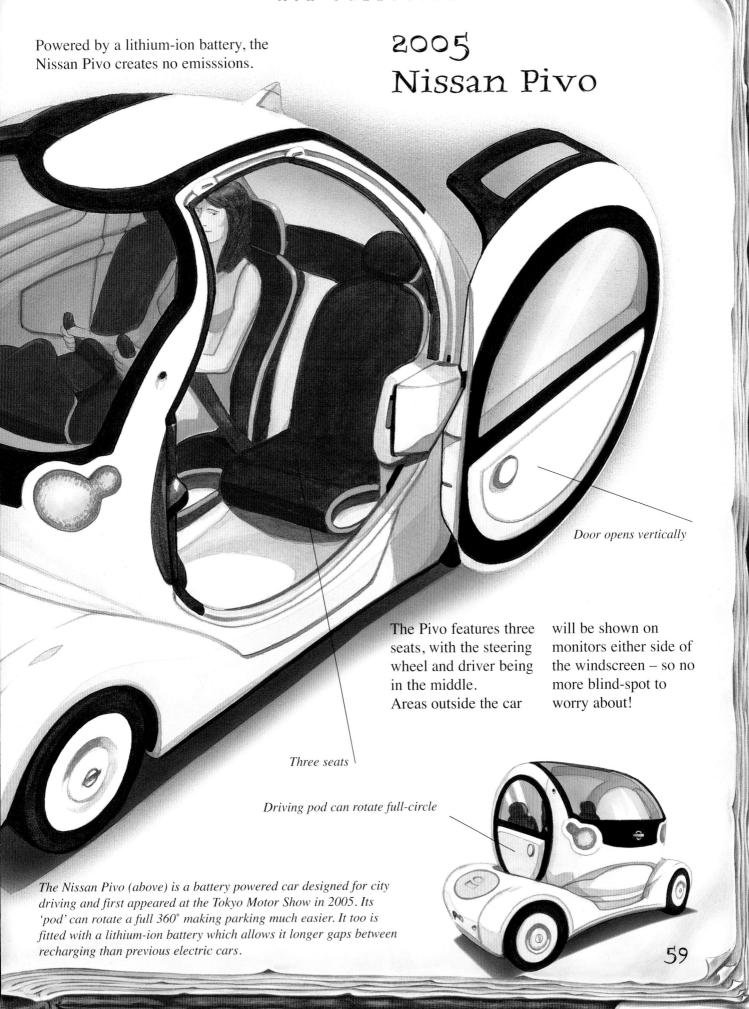

Door opens vertically

The Pivo features three seats, with the steering wheel and driver being in the middle. Areas outside the car will be shown on monitors either side of the windscreen – so no more blind-spot to worry about!

Three seats

Driving pod can rotate full-circle

The Nissan Pivo (above) is a battery powered car designed for city driving and first appeared at the Tokyo Motor Show in 2005. Its 'pod' can rotate a full 360° making parking much easier. It too is fitted with a lithium-ion battery which allows it longer gaps between recharging than previous electric cars.

INTO THE FUTURE

Mountain bike

What will land transport be like in the future? At the beginning of the 20th century few people realised the noisy, unreliable vehicles that occasionally appeared on roads would take over from horses and carts or carriages. A hundred years from now will people look back and say "Weren't those people at the beginning of the 21st century silly not to realise that vehicles with petrol engines would be replaced by...?" By what? That's the problem facing governments and traffic planners: just what **is** going to replace such vehicles? They certainly need replacing – they cause pollution, congestion and consume fossil fuels – but they also provide convenient, flexible transport that no railway can match. The illustrations on this spread suggest some future transport possibilities.

Materials

New materials will also affect transport. Carbon-fibre, first used in racing bikes, is light and thin, but also rigid and very strong. Stronger and tougher tyres led to the popularity of the mountain bike (top left) for leisure cycling.

Toyota Prius

Hybrid (electric-petrol) cars use a NiMH (nickel-metal-hydride) battery as well as a small petrol motor. When the car doesn't need much power e.g. going downhill or driving slowly, the petrol motor switches off. At high speed the two engines work together, and when the car brakes, the force used to slow the car down, recharges the battery.

Hybrid cars

*Maglev train
(magnetic levitation)*

The future?

The shape of transport to come? In theory, Maglev trains (top), hovering over and propelled by huge magnetic coils, will travel at up to 700 km/h. Unfortunately, in practice, this system is incredibly expensive to build and operate because it uses so much electricity. In fact Germany dropped plans to build a Maglev railway because of the expense. Vehicles fitted with solar panels store energy for later use - for example at night. Getting lost or struggling with maps will also be a thing of the past when all vehicles are fitted with Sat Nav (satellite navigation).

Solar power

Sunraycer (below) runs on 1000 watts of solar power, but can only carry one person.

*Silicon solar
cells*

Glossary

articulated truck (artic) truck with two separate parts: the front traction unit and the rear trailer unit.

axle rod around which a wheel rotates. In older vehicles and railway wagons, it was a shaft, rod or beam joining a pair of wheels.

camber convex surface of a road, with the centre higher than the sides so water drains off the road quickly.

carbon dioxide a colourless gas naturally present in the atmosphere, and also created by burning fossil fuels.

carbon-fibre thin strands of pure carbon used to reinforce moulded plastic articles, making them much stronger and lighter than metal ones.

chassis a vehicle's frame (distinct from the bodywork) to which the engine and gearbox are fitted.

cylinder metal tube inside an engine where the fuel is burned.

fossil fuels fuels formed deep underground from decayed plants and animals, for example coal, oil and gas.

gear machinery in a car or truck which lets the driver control the engine's power and vehicle's speed.

horsepower unit for measuring the power of an engine, first worked out by James Watt (1736-1819).

hub centre of a wheel which rotates around the axle.

hydrocarbons compounds of hydrogen and carbon. They are the main components of petrol.

internal combustion engine engine in which the fuel burns in the cylinder – in a steam engine it burns in the firebox.

Maglev 'magnetic levitation', a system of transport using electricity and huge magnetic coils to power specially designed electric trains.

mass production technique of making things in large numbers, so making them cheaper.

nitrogen oxides name given to a group of gases containing nitrogen and oxygen. They are mainly produced by petrol-burning vehicles.

pack animal animal that carries goods on its back.

pantograph frame on top of an electric locomotive or tram through which electricity passes from overhead cables to the vehicle.

piston disc that slides up and down inside an engine's cylinder.

pneumatic something, like a tyre, that can be blown up with compressed air.

prototype first, or original, model of a vehicle used to test its design to make sure everything works properly before it goes into production.

Sat Nav (satellite navigation) in-car navigation device using data from satellites to provide directions and traffic information direct to vehicles.

shafts horizontal poles on a coach or cart between which the horse stands. The poles support the horse-collar.

tire metal band fitted around a wheel rim to strengthen it.

tractor unit smaller front part of an artic, with the engine and driver's cab.

trailer unit larger rear part of an artic. It is pulled by the tractor and carries the load.

transverse engine engine which lies from wheel to wheel instead of from the front to the back of a car.

valve part of an engine that regulates the flow of fuel and air into and out of an engine's cylinders.

velocipede term for any early bicycle with pedals.

Index

SALARIYA

Published in Great Britain in 2006 by
Book House, an imprint of
The Salariya Book Company Ltd
25 Marlborough Place, Brighton, BN1 1UB

Please visit the Salariya Book Company at:
www.salariya.com for free electronic versions of:

You Wouldn't Want to Be a Roman Gladiator!
You Wouldn't Want to Be an Egyptian Mummy!
Avoid joining Shackleton's Polar Expedition!

HB ISBN-10: 1-905087-89-6
HB ISBN-13: 978-1-905087-89-1
PB ISBN-10: 1-905087-90-X
PB ISBN-13: 978-1-905087-90-7

Editor: Sophie Izod
Editorial Assistant: Mark Williams
Illustrated by: David Antram, Mark Peppé, John James, Mark
Bergin, Gerald Wood, Nick Hewetson, Tony Townsend, James
Field, Gordon Davies, Carolyn Scrace